Crime-fighting

Chris Oxlade

First published in Great Britain by Heinemann Library
Halley Court, Jordan Hill, Oxford OX2 8EJ
a division of Reed Educational & Professional Publishing Ltd

OXFORD FLORENCE PRAGUE MADRID ATHENS MELBOURNE AUCKLAND
KUALA LUMPUR SINGAPORE TOKYO IBADAN NAIROBI KAMPALA
JOHANNESBURG GABORONE PORTSMOUTH NH (USA) CHICAGO MEXICO
CITY SAO PAULO

00 99 98 97 96
10 9 8 7 6 5 4 3 2 1

ISBN 0 431 06446 6

Designed by **AMR**
Illustrations by Art Construction
Originated in the UK by Dot Gradations Ltd, Wickford.
Printed and bound in the UK by Jarrold Printing Ltd, Thetford.

British Library Cataloguing in Publication Data
Oxlade, Chris
   Crime fighting. – (Making science work)
   1. Criminal investigation – Juvenile literature 2. Forensic sciences – Juvenile literature
   I. Title
   363.2'5
A catalogue record for this book is available from the British Library

Acknowledgements
The publishers would like to thank the following for permission to reproduce
photographs.

Peter Menzel/Science Photo Library: p.4; Associated Press/Topham: p.5; James King-
Holmes/Science Photo Library: p.10; Image Bank: p.11; Philippe Plailly/Science Photo
Library: p.12; Michael Gilbert/Science Photo Library: p.15; Gary S Chapman/Image
Bank: p.16; Andrew Syred/Science Photo Library: p.17; Shout: p.18; Harvey
Pincis/Science Photo Library: p.20; Press Association/Topham: p.21; Alfred
Gescheidt/Image Bank: p.23; Kay Chernush/Image Bank; p.24; Will & Deni
McIntyre/Science Photo Library: p.25; Scott Camazine/Science Photo Library: p.26; R
Drexel/Bilderberg/Network: p.27; Topham: p.28, p.29; Ander McIntyre: p.7, p.8, p.9,
p.22.

Cover photograph reproduced with the permission of Alfred Pasieka/Science Photo
Library.

Our thanks to Jim Drake for his comments in the preparation of this book.

The publishers have made every effort to trace copyright holders. However, if any
material has been incorrectly acknowledged, we should be pleased to correct this at the
earliest opportunity.

CONTENTS

SCIENCE IN CRIME FIGHTING

How many examples of the police using science can you think of? It may be only one or two, and fingerprinting is probably one of them! In fact, the police use many areas of science, including physics, chemistry and biology. In this book, you can find out how science can be used to help prevent crime in the first place, and how it can help solve crimes after they have happened.

Crime prevention

It is much better to prevent a crime than to spend time and money investigating it afterwards, perhaps without success. Police officers and security people use science for surveillance (watching and listening) and to catch criminals as they are carrying out crimes. For example, in a shopping centre, security cameras watch all the customers in case someone tries to steal from one of the shops. Other examples of where science helps to prevent crime include burglar alarms and **X-ray** machines, which search luggage for suspicious objects.

Evidence collected from crime scenes is processed in a forensic science laboratory.

Forensic science

Forensic science is the use of science to help solve a crime that has taken place. Forensic scientists work in laboratories, analysing evidence from the scene of a crime. They try to match the evidence from the scene with evidence from any suspects. These forensic clues are vital pieces in the jigsaw of finding the criminal. For example, tiny pieces of paint found under a suspect's fingernails might match the paint from a crime scene.

Forensic scientists present their evidence to law courts where criminals are tried for their crimes. These scientists are called expert witnesses because they are experts on the evidence they are presenting.

Taking care of the evidence

Every item of forensic evidence must be looked after carefully, from the time it is found to the time when it is presented in court. A record is kept of every person who handles the evidence. This is to prevent anyone from interfering with it.

Forensic evidence is presented in law courts during trials. Witnesses will be asked questions relating to the evidence.

SECURITY SCIENCE

Science does not just help to catch criminals – it also helps to stop crime happening in the first place. You have probably seen security devices such as video cameras and burglar alarms at your school, in local shops or even at home. Security devices help to deter criminals from carrying out break-ins or stealing goods. They can also help the police to catch criminals actually carrying out the crimes.

Burglar alarms

A burglar alarm system protects a home, a school, a factory or other building from being broken into when it is empty, for example at night or during a weekend. When the system is switched on, it automatically senses if any doors or windows are opened, and if people are walking through the rooms. If the system detects such movement, it sets off an alarm.

Magnetic devices called sensors can detect if doors or windows are opened. When the door is closed, a magnetically operated electric switch in the door frame keeps it closed. When the door opens, the switch also opens. This is detected by the alarm's control panel. An infra-red sensor detects moving bodies in a room or corridor. Rays of infra-red radiation are given off by all warm things. An infra-red sensor looks for any infra-red radiation coming from a room. If the source of the radiation moves, it sends a signal to the control panel and the alarm is set off.

The type of infra-red sensor used in domestic burglar alarms. The sensor can 'see' a much wider area than a human eye.

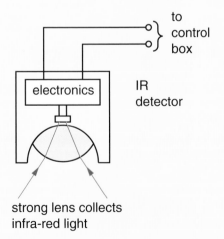

Open — magnet — connects to control box

Closed — to control box

to control box

electronics — IR detector

strong lens collects infra-red light

Electronic locks

Electronic locks stop unauthorized people from entering a room or building. They are much more difficult to break open than ordinary locks with keys. To open an electronic lock, you have to tap in the correct sequence of numbers on a keypad. Some locks work with a credit card-like key which you 'swipe' past the lock to open it. Other lock systems can examine fingerprints or voice prints, and will allow in only those ones that they recognize. A voice print is a record of the mixture of sounds in a person's voice. No two voice prints are the same.

This security camera keeps a watchful eye over a busy town centre road. Many kinds of criminal activity can be recorded and the criminals identified.

Closed-circuit television

Closed-circuit television cameras keep watch over shops, banks and busy streets. Sometimes the pictures from the cameras are watched on screens by security guards. In other systems, the pictures are recorded onto video tape. Later, the tape is played back so that any criminal suspects can be identified if a crime has happened.

ELECTRONIC TAGS

Many clothing shops have electronic tagging machines to stop customers from stealing clothes. Each item in the shop has a tag attached to it. If somebody takes a garment out of the shop without paying for it, a sensor at the door detects the electronic tag and sets off an alarm.

STOPPING FRAUD AND FORGERY

If you cheat somebody out of money, for example by using their credit card, then you commit a crime called **fraud**. **Forgery** is a crime that involves making something, such as a bank note, which appears to be real but is not. So how does science help to prevent fraud and forgery?

Security codes

Security codes are used to stop anyone from using other people's bank accounts or looking at computer records without permission. Most security codes consist of a list of numbers or letters. For example, to get money from a bank cash machine, you need to type in your own personal identification number (PIN). To look at some computer records you have to enter a password first.

In the future you will not need to give an automatic teller machine (cashpoint) a security code. It may be able to recognise your face automatically.

This forged signature has taken a lot of practice. Look how similar the signatures are.

Signature checks

The most common way of preventing fraud in shops and banks is to ask a person to sign their name. This is then compared to the signature already on the person's bank card or credit card. Sometimes, the signature on the card is printed in invisible ink. It only shows up when the ink is lit up by **ultra-violet light** from a special lamp. This is designed to stop criminals from copying the signature.

Bank notes and credit cards

There are many ways to make it more difficult for criminals to forge bank notes and bank cards. Bank notes are printed with many different colours of ink, and the lines which make up the pictures are very fine. This makes the notes difficult to print without the use of very expensive machinery. Some bank notes have a thin metal strip that is made of a mixture of different metals. The metals in the strip can be tested to find out if the note is genuine. Bank cards often have **holograms** on them. You need very complicated equipment to make a hologram, so these cards are difficult to copy.

MOBILE PHONES

When you use a mobile telephone, it sends a security code to the telephone exchange. The exchange needs the correct code before it lets the user make a call. Unfortunately, criminals can detect the radio signals from some mobile phones and copy the signals into stolen phones. All the call charges from the stolen phone are then sent to the person using the real phone.

CRIME ON THE MOVE

S cience helps to catch people who are breaking the law as they travel around the country or the world. With the help of **X-rays** and magnetism, security machines can find hidden things, such as illegal firearms, in luggage or clothing. Radar devices can trap and record motorists who are breaking the speed limit. It is even possible to keep track of exactly where a stolen car is being driven to.

Airport security

Airport security checks try to prevent people from carrying guns or explosives onto aircraft, where they could be used in a hijack. All luggage is passed through an X-ray scanner before it goes onto the aircraft. X-rays pass right through most materials, but dense materials like metals stop them. When X-rays are sent through a bag with a gun inside it, this makes the outline of the gun show up.

Passengers cannot go through an airport X-ray machine because too many X-rays can harm your body. Instead, passengers walk through a metal detector, which detects any large pieces of metal they might be carrying in their pockets, such as a gun or dangerous knife. A metal detector works by setting up a **magnetic field** (like the one around a magnet). Any metal which enters the magnetic field changes the field's shape. This change is detected by the machine's electronics and an alarm is set off.

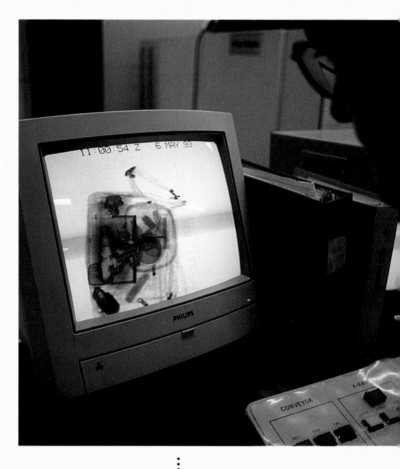

An X-ray scanner operator looks for signs of suspicious objects in a shoulder bag.

A speed camera looking for cars travelling faster than the speed limit on an urban road. It measures the speed as the car approaches.

FOLLOW THAT CAR!

It is possible to have a tracking device hidden inside a car. If the car is reported as stolen, a radio signal is sent out from a tracking station. This turns on the tracking device in the car, which begins to send out its own signal. The police can then follow the signal to find the stolen car.

Radar guns

A speed 'gun' works out the speed of a vehicle which is moving towards it or away from it. It works by radar, which is short for *r*adio *d*etection *a*nd *r*anging. Radar sends out radio waves and detects any which bounce back. The time it takes for the waves to travel back tells the machine how far away a vehicle is. By taking two readings a split second apart, the machine can work out the vehicle's speed. Roadside speed cameras have a built-in radar gun. They automatically take a photograph of any cars which are breaking the speed limit. The owner can be traced from the car's licence plate.

THE SCENE OF A CRIME

The police know that even the most cunning criminals often leave behind signs that they have been at the scene of a crime. These signs are called evidence. The police use evidence to try to track down the guilty person. As soon as the police arrive at the scene of a crime, they make sure that nothing is moved. Then the scene is photographed, and the exact position of all the evidence is measured and noted down. Finally, the evidence is collected. Some pieces of evidence are so small that they can be seen only with a **microscope**.

Finding prints

Fingerprints are some of the most important clues that forensic scientists can find. Fingerprints are normally invisible, but they show up when you dust them with fine powder. Then they can be transferred to sticky tape and photographed. At the crime scene, all the possible places where the criminal could have left fingerprints are examined.

....
Brushing surfaces with fine magnetic powder makes any fingerprints show up.

Collecting other evidence

Investigators wear gloves to collect evidence, so that they do not put their own fingerprints on it. Small items of evidence, such as pieces of glass, hairs, fibres from fabrics and pieces of soil, are sucked into a vacuum cleaner and trapped in a **filter**. Small samples of blood stains are collected on **swabs**. Every piece of evidence is put into its own separate plastic bag and carefully labelled to prevent getting mixed up with other items.

A murder scene

At the scene of a murder, the position of the dead person's body is photographed, measured and marked. Then the body is taken away for specialists to try to work out when and how the person died. Sometimes a body is found years after the person has died, and only the skeleton is left. In this case, specialists have to work out who the person was, as well as how they died.

PLASTER PRINTS

Fingerprints are not the only prints that forensic scientists look for. They also collect footprints and tyre tracks from vehicles. A copy of the print or track is made by pouring **plaster** into it and letting the plaster set. The scientists try to match the prints to the shoes or vehicles of possible suspects.

The outline on the ground shows where a body was found.

FINGERPRINTS

There are billions of people in the world, but do you know what makes you different from all those other people? The answer is your fingerprints. They are unique. Nobody else in the world has fingerprints with the same pattern of lines as yours. Every time you touch something, you leave your fingerprints on it (unless you are wearing gloves). Fingerprints are the best way of identifying people. The police can use them to find out who has been at the scene of a crime.

Leaving fingerprints

Fingerprints are caused by the ridges and furrows on your fingertips. If your fingers have dirt or paint on them, they leave prints which can easily be seen and photographed. Even if your fingers are clean, they still leave traces of sweat and natural oils which are always on your skin. These fingerprints can be found by brushing them with fine powder which sticks to the sweat and oil. Fingerprints on paper and cloth are made to show up by using special chemicals (see page 18). Some fingerprints can only be seen by shining **laser light** on them.

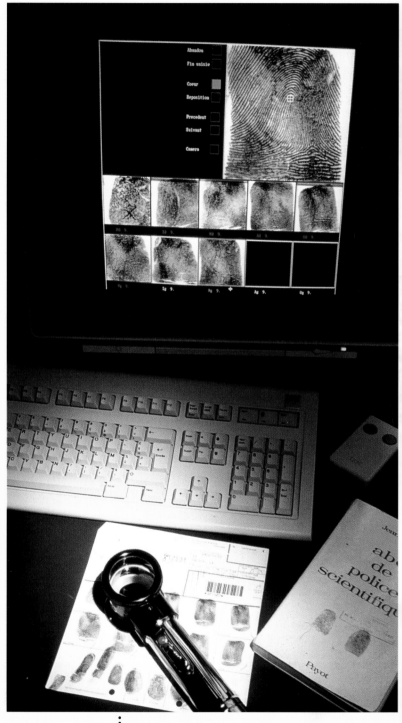

Studying fingerprints records on paper and computer.

Fingerprint records

The police make fingerprint records of all the people who could possibly have been at the scene of the crime, even if they know the people have nothing to do with the crime. Any fingerprints found at the scene which match these people's fingerprints can then be ignored. This may leave unknown fingerprints which could belong to the criminal. The fingerprints of people who have a criminal record (have been convicted for crimes they have committed before) are stored in computer **databases**.

Which shapes?

Fingerprint experts group fingerprints according to their patterns. Common shapes in fingerprints are loops, whorls and arches. By classifying fingerprints in this way the police can match fingerprints found at the scene of a crime with ones that they have on their records.

MILLIONS OF PRINTS

In the 1880s, a British scientist, Sir Francis Galton (1822–1911), realized that no two people have the same fingerprints. Fingerprinting became a police method soon after. The British police now have about 4 million fingerprint records, and the FBI, which investigates crimes in the United States, has about 80 million.

Although people have similar fingerprint patterns, no two people have exactly the same ones.

CLUES IN YOUR BODY

As well as fingerprinting, there are other ways of matching a person to evidence that they leave behind at the scene of a crime. Specks of blood and hairs are especially useful. The blood samples are tested, and skin and hair samples are analysed and then compared to samples taken from suspects.

Blood groups

Scientists divide human blood into different types, called blood groups. A blood test works out which group a specimen of blood belongs to. When a suspect's blood type matches that of a blood sample from a crime scene, it cannot prove anything because millions of other people will have the same blood group. However, if no match in the blood groups is found, the police can eliminate a suspect from their enquiries.

What is DNA?

DNA stands for deoxyribonucleic acid. It is a chemical which is found in almost every **cell** in every living thing. DNA is like a recipe for making a person. Everybody's DNA recipe is slightly different, except for identical twins! The pattern of your DNA determines the colour of your hair and eyes, and almost everything else about your body. DNA is passed from parents to children, which is why you may look like your father or mother.

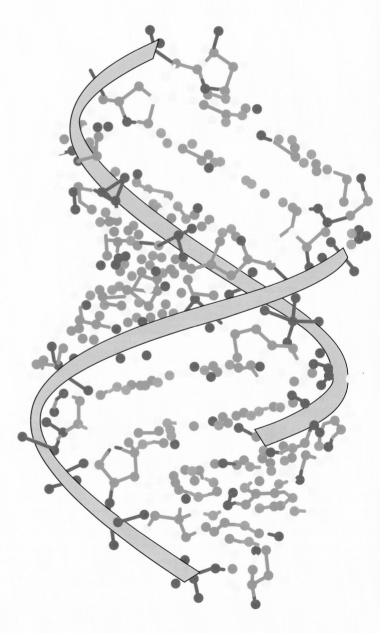

DNA is very complicated. The DNA in every cell contains millions of atoms.

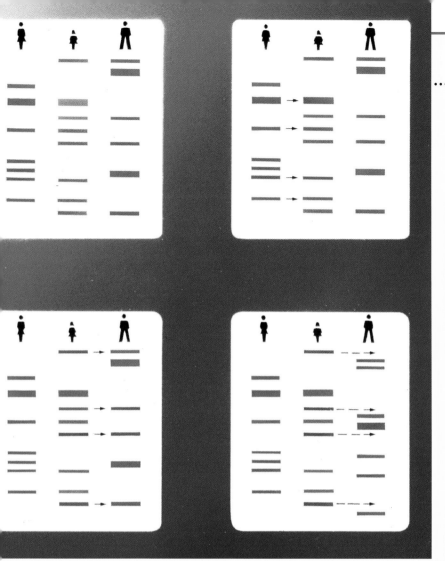

Each picture shows three DNA samples (from a woman, a child and a man). The first three show that the child has inherited some DNA from each of its parents. The man in the last picture cannot be the child's father.

Making a DNA profile

A DNA profile is made using samples collected from a crime scene. It is a chart which shows whether certain pieces are present in a person's DNA. The process of making a DNA profile is very complicated, and it needs specialized laboratory equipment. A profile can only be made from cells, and they must be quite fresh. Because hair itself is dead, a hair with a root is needed for a DNA profile. Red blood cells contain no DNA, so only white blood cells can be used. A finished profile is a long strip of photographic film with light and dark bands across it. If the patterns of light and dark on two profiles match, then there is a very good chance that the two samples of DNA came from the same person.

FINGERPRINTS ARE BEST!

Although no two people have the same DNA (except for identical twins), it is possible that the DNA profiles of two people could look the same. So although DNA profiling is a very useful test, it is not as reliable as a good fingerprint!

MICROSCOPIC EVIDENCE

Criminals do not always leave a convenient fingerprint at the scene of a crime! So forensic scientists also look for other evidence which will help them to trace the criminal. One method is to study fragments of evidence from the scene, and try to match them with something belonging to a suspect. For example, a tiny fibre of cloth could be matched to clothes found at a suspect's house, or a bullet could be matched to a gun found with a suspect's fingerprints on it. To make these matches, scientists have to examine the evidence under a microscope in the forensic laboratory.

Forensic ballistics

Ballistics is the science of how bullets (and bombs and missiles) are fired, and how they travel through the air. The study of forensic ballistics helps the police to match a bullet with the gun from which it was fired. When a bullet is fired, it gets bumped and scratched by the gun. Every gun leaves its own particular set of marks on a bullet, rather like a fingerprint. In the laboratory, bullets are studied under a bullet-comparison microscope.

In a similar way, the marks and wounds made by other weapons, such as knives and even human teeth, can also be studied under a microscope. They can be matched to the weapon that made them, or to the set of teeth that made the bite!

These unused bullets are unmarked. As soon as they are fired, they can be traced to the gun that fired them.

Examining the evidence

The fragments that are found at the scene of a crime are often mixed together. In the laboratory, hairs, fibres, bits of paint, wood and glass are separated and examined using a **binocular microscope**. This is really two microscopes – one for each eye – that are placed side by side. A binocular microscope allows you to see objects magnified and in three dimensions.

Most substances which are not from living things are made up of crystals. Forensic scientists use a **polarizing microscope** to help identify crystals, such as drugs. The polarizing microscope makes different crystals show up in different colours.

A photomicrograph (photograph from a microscope) of two different types of fibre. The fibres may have looked the same to the naked eye.

FORGED PAPERS

Like fingers and bullets, typewriters leave their own 'fingerprints' on paper. This may happen because a letter is slightly worn down. Many criminals have been caught because the police have been able to match forged paperwork to the typewriter on which it was typed.

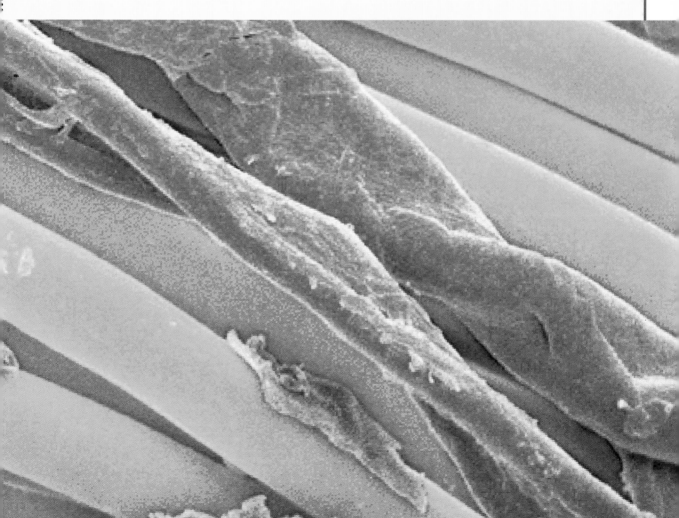

CHEMICAL EVIDENCE

Vital evidence is often present at a crime scene, but it is invisible to the naked eye. So how do forensic scientists find it? The answer is by carrying out chemical tests. Some tests make hidden clues show up. Other tests show which chemicals are in a sample of evidence. Chemical tests may destroy the actual evidence, so forensic scientists only use a small sample of a piece of evidence for their tests.

Uncovering forgeries

Gas **chromatography** is a process which shows the chemicals in a sample, and how much of each chemical the sample contains. It is used to test whether things which look the same are really made of the same substance. For example, a forged credit card may look the same as a real one, but it might be made of a slightly different sort of plastic. A test in a gas chromatograph machine would show up the difference. A breath-test machine is a special sort of chromatograph which detects the amount of alcohol there is in a person's breath. It is used to find out whether a driver has drunk more alcohol than is allowed by law.

This driver has been stopped by the police and asked to take a breath-test. If the test proves that the driver has drunk more alcohol than is permitted before driving, there will be a severe penalty.

Hidden fingerprints

Fingerprints on rough surfaces, such as paper and cloth, cannot be seen by dusting them with powder (see page 12). Instead, the piece of paper or cloth has to be soaked in a special chemical called ninhydrin. The ninhydrin reacts with the chemicals in the sweat on the fingerprint. This makes new chemicals, which show up in a dark colour to make the fingerprint pattern appear.

How to compare substances

Spectrophotometry is another way of testing to see if two substances are the same. A spectrophotometer is an instrument which detects light rays which are invisible to our eyes, so it can see differences between substances which we cannot see. For example, a spectrophotometer might be able to spot the difference between two types of black paint.

Ninhydrin testing reveals fingerprints that might not show up during tests with powder.

TEST RESULTS

The results from a gas chromatograph test can be compared with information about thousands of different products. The information is supplied by the product manufacturers. For example, when the police find a forged credit card, with the help of a gas chromatograph test, they may be able to tell which factory the card's plastic was made in. The factory can then give the police a list of the people who bought that particular plastic.

MEDICAL EVIDENCE

Forensic medicine is the branch of medicine which investigates any suspicious deaths. It helps the police to work out how the person died, and exactly when the death took place. Even if the cause of a person's death seems obvious, forensic scientists look carefully at the body because there may be other, hidden injuries that are not obvious at first. The body of a dead person is taken from the scene of a crime to a **pathology** laboratory for examination.

Tools of the trade

In the pathology laboratory, a forensic pathologist studies the body to find out how the person died. This process is called an autopsy, or post-mortem examination. The pathologist makes notes of any marks and wounds on the outside of the body, and takes photographs of them. Then the body's internal **organs** are examined. Other specialists may be called in to help, such as a forensic toxicologist who looks for evidence of poisons or drugs in the body. Any pieces of bullet or knife that are found in the body are removed and used to help the police find the murder weapon.

A forensic pathologist studying samples of body tissues in a pathology laboratory.

These murder weapons, seized soon after a terrorist attack, will be examined for clues that link them to the attack and the victims' injuries.

When did the person die?

It is often just as important to work out when a person died as to discover how they died. If a suspect was seen away from the scene of the murder at the time of death, then they cannot be the murderer. After a person dies, the body temperature begins to fall. A few hours later, their muscles begin to stiffen. These are clues to the time of death. If a person has been dead for a few days before being discovered, their body begins to rot. A pathologist estimates how long the person has been dead by the amount of **decomposition** in the body.

INSECT CLUES

Forensic entomologists (scientists who study insects) study the maggots which feed on dead bodies. The age of the maggots gives a good clue to how long ago the person died. The particular species of maggot can even show scientists in which area of the country the person died.

WHOSE BODY?

It may take months, or even years, before a dead person's body is discovered. Only the skeleton may be left, so how do the police work out who the person was, or how they died? They call in forensic scientists who specialize in finding clues from dead bodies. The scientists study the body's skeleton and teeth, and try to build up a file of information about the person.

Dental records

The best clue to a person's identity is their teeth. The size of the teeth, and how much they have decayed (rotted), can indicate the person's sex and age. Any dental work on the teeth, such as fillings or false teeth, can also be matched with the dental records of missing people. The use of teeth in this way is called forensic odontology.

Skeleton clues

A skeleton can provide an amazing amount of information about a person. Investigations of skeletons are carried out by forensic anthropologists, who have specialist knowledge of skeletons and how they grow. The person's sex and race can be worked out from the shape of the skull and the pelvis. The person's age can be estimated by looking at those areas of the bones where growth takes place.

Even if only a few bones of a skeleton are found, the person's height can be estimated. The length and width of the bones are carefully measured and used to calculate the probable height. The femur (the upper leg bone) is the most useful bone to find because it is the longest in the body.

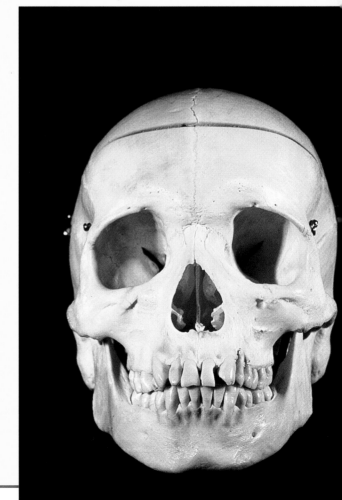

Forensic scientists can identify bodies that have been dead for so long that only a skeleton is left. Investigating the teeth, or building a face shape (right) can reveal a person's age, sex, name, and sometimes the way they died.

Model skulls

Forensic anthropologists can use a skull to get an idea of what the dead person's face looked like when they were alive. A copy is made of the person's skull, and then clay is used to build up the flesh areas on the model. The thickness of flesh changes over different parts of the face, and the model-maker uses this knowledge to build a good likeness of the dead person. Pictures of the finished model are shown to the public, to find out if anyone recognizes the face.

BONE FACTS

It is not always easy or accurate to estimate a person's age from individual bones. On average, men are taller than women, and various factors, such as diet and environment, can affect a person's height. Also, we all begin to shrink by about 0.5 mm a year after the age of thirty!

This face superimposed on a skull shows how the shape of the face depends on the skull.

TRUE OR FALSE?

After the police have arrested a suspect, they may use certain tests to find out whether the suspect is telling them the truth or lying. They can use another test to find out if the suspect is mentally ill. A different type of test can be used to find handwriting clues on what look like blank sheets of paper. These tests are carried out by specially trained scientists.

Lie detectors

A lie detector test does exactly what you might think – it tries to show whether a suspect is telling the truth. A lie detector machine (sometimes called a polygraph) measures a person's **pulse rate**, **blood pressure**, breathing rate and how much they sweat. It then prints the results on paper. At the same time as the machine makes these measurements, the person is asked questions. If the person lies, their pulse rate, breathing rate and so on are likely to change. Any changes will show up on the machine. In some countries evidence from lie detectors can be used in court cases. In many other countries, however, the authorities do not believe that the tests are reliable enough.

Sensors attached to the man's body send information to the lie detector. There is a line on the paper for each sensor.

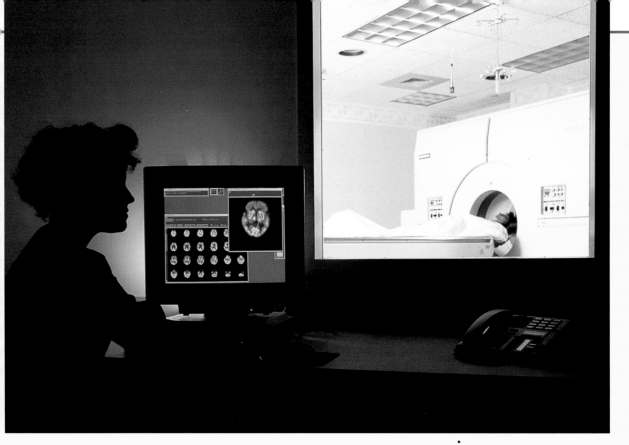

A patient
undergoing a
brain scan. Cross-
sections of the
head appear on
the computer
screen.

Brain scans

In some cases, murderers plead insanity as a defence, saying
that they did not know that they were doing something wrong.
In a few cases, the murderer is given a brain scan to check the
state of their brain. This is done by a machine called a PET
scanner. It produces pictures of the chemical activity in the
brain. A **neurologist** may be able to spot any brain problems
from the scan. If a problem is noticed, then it is possible that
the suspect may have committed the crime without really
understanding that they were doing something wrong.

ESDA test

Imagine that a person has written a forged letter on a pad of
notepaper, and sent the letter in the post. If there are no
fingerprints on the paper, how can the police find out where it
came from? An ESDA (electrostatic detection apparatus) test
might help. It will show up what was written on the sheets of
paper which have already been torn off the pad. It does this by
showing up the tiny dents in the pad that were made by a pen
moving across the sheets of paper. The dents show up in black,
like the writing on a photocopy.

COMPUTERS IN CRIME FIGHTING

Police forces around the world use computers more and more in their work. Computers are very good at storing huge amounts of information in **databases**, and searching through that information to match, for example, a fingerprint or some other evidence. Police computers hold information about criminals (their name, any aliases, photograph, any previous convictions for crimes and so on), fingerprint records and information about particular cases they have investigated previously. Computers search through the database to find matches with evidence.

Fingerprint databases

Most police forces keep fingerprint records on computer. Fingerprints of convicted criminals are entered into the computer with a machine called a scanner. The computer will have a 'picture' of every fingerprint that has been scanned in this way. Information about the fingerprint shapes and sizes is also added. The computer operator uses this information to try to help the police find a match with any unidentified fingerprints found at a crime scene. Any close matches can be shown on the computer screen next to the unidentified print. The computer can search for a fingerprint in seconds, whereas it would take a person many hours to do the same search.

....

This fingerprint has been scanned onto a computer. If fingerprints are found at a crime scene, they too are scanned, and the computer can check very quickly through its databases to see if there is a recorded match.

Photofit pictures

A photofit is a picture of someone's face that is made from a witness's description. The photofit may be a picture of a suspect, a murder victim or even a missing person. Photofits are made using computer graphics. The witness sits with the computer artist, picking out different shapes and colours of nose, mouth, eyes and so on from a series of pictures. In this way, they gradually build up a face. The computer artist can adjust the face in any way with electronic pens and paintbrushes. The completed photofit picture is printed and used on crime posters.

What is image enhancement?

As well as helping to build up pictures of faces, computers can be used to make photographs more clear. This is called image enhancement. A blurred or fuzzy picture is first scanned into the computer. The computer operator then tries to work out what the original picture would have looked like. Image enhancement can make a suspect's face clear enough to recognize, or a car number plate readable.

This photofit will be put on public display, to help jog the memory of people who may have spotted a criminal in action. They might be able to help the police catch the criminal.

WHOSE FACE?

In the future, computers may be able to find faces in photographs or clips of film from a video camera. They could then automatically match the face with photographs in a database of people with a criminal record.

GLOSSARY

binocular microscope a microscope with two sets of lenses – one for each eye – that are placed side by side. It allows you to see objects magnified and in three dimensions.

blood pressure measures how well your heart pumps blood around your body

cell the basic building block of all animals and plants. There are hundreds of different types of cell. Each type does its own special job.

chromatography a method that separates the different substances in a mixture

database a store of information held on a computer. The information is arranged so that it is easy for the computer to search through it.

decomposition the process in which the remains of animals and plants break down into other chemicals. It is caused by tiny living things, such as bacteria.

filter a screen with tiny holes in it. It stops particles bigger than a certain size passing through it. The holes can be microscopically small.

forgery any object (for example a document, a ticket, a bank note, or a painting) which looks like the real thing but is only a copy

fraud a crime in which people make money by lying or using forged documents, for example using a forged credit card

hologram a special kind of photograph that produces a three-dimensional picture when lit up

laser a very strong, narrow beam of light. Very powerful lasers can cut through metal.

magnetic field the space around a magnet where the magnet's pull can be felt

microscope an instrument which makes tiny things look much bigger. You look at the things through an eyepiece. There are several different types of microscope.

neurologist a doctor who specializes in studying the brain and nervous system

organ a part of the body which does a particular job, such as the stomach, the heart or the lungs

pathology the study of diseases and their effect on the human body

plaster a mixture of powder and water which can be moulded into shape and then left to set solid

polarizing microscope a microscope that makes tiny crystals of different substances show up in different colours

pulse rate the number of times your heart beats every minute

spectrophotometry a method of working out which chemicals are in a substance. This is done by measuring how the substance gives off different colours of light.

swab a piece of material that soaks up liquid. Swabs are used to collect liquid evidence, such as blood.

ultra-violet light a type of light that our eyes cannot detect. When it hits some substances, it makes them give off light that we can see.

X-rays rays of light that can pass through less dense substances, such as skin. They are stopped by more dense substances, such as metals.

FACTFILE

- The famous artist Leonardo da Vinci often smoothed paint with his fingers. His fingerprints show up on some of his paintings, and can be used to identify fake paintings.

- Most burglar alarms have a four-digit security code. The number is entered on a keypad with the digits 0 to 9. If a burglar tried to guess the code, they would have a 10,000 to 1 chance of getting it right.

- A night terror is a dream during which a person becomes violent and may kill somebody, without knowing what they are doing. Suspects sometimes claim in their defence that they suffer from night terror. Their brain activity is measured during sleep to see if it is abnormal.

- Forensic ballistics can show the place where a bullet was fired from, as well as which gun fired it.

- DNA profiling is used to link people to other people as well as people to evidence. It can prove, for example, that two people are related to each other.

- Martin Tytell, who lives and works in New York, is known as Mr Typewriter. If you give him a sheet of paper with typing on it, he can probably name the exact model of typewriter that produced it.

- Satellites in space can see and photograph some types of illegal activity on the Earth's surface. One example is their use to spot fields of drugs being grown in remote mountains or jungles.

INDEX